Not Looking For Signs

Belinda Broughton
Not Looking For Signs

Acknowledgements

Thank you to

Everyone who has ever encouraged my poetry – so many of you, but especially (for this publication): Louise Nicholas, Rachael Mead, Hana Broughton, Ervin Janek and Graham Rowlands

FabriK, Lobethal, SA

Jo Wilmot (creator of Solastalgia, the exhibition)
and the team in Tall Trees and Understories

Not Looking For Signs
ISBN 978 1 76041 862 5
Copyright © text Belinda Broughton 2020
Copyright © illustrations Belinda Broughton 2020
Cover design: Hana Broughton

First published 2020 by
Ginninderra Press
PO Box 3461 Port Adelaide 5015
www.ginninderrapress.com.au

Contents

Foreword	7
the flight of the wild swan	11
Blackbird in Honeysuckle	13
One Gift	15
White Crow	17
The Empty Man	18
weep tears, shed blood	19
To God	21
I'm Angry with God Again	23
Always Cockroaches	25
reminiscence from a barren planet	27
after fire, Katarapko	29
Our Hold on the Planet	31
Sketching Drought	32
Little Snatch of Darkness	33
two gods	35
Owl at Dusk	37
Not Looking for Signs	39
impossible spring	41
hopeful songs	42
Summer Dream	43
Adelaide Hills, January 2015	45
Meeting the Spirit of the River Murray	46
Each Day	49
Come Forest	51
What the Dreamed Man Gave	53
Unexpected Lecture on Global Warming from a Bird	55
The Original Song	57
what matters	58

A Transparent Matter	59
Blue Wren Fights His Reflection	60
in the waterhole	63

Foreword

'Tall Trees and Understories is the chosen theme for the fourth iteration of the touring exhibition Solastalgia, a platform for artists and communities regionally (South Australia) to reclaim hope for the places we love, evoking our compassion for the earth in crisis, our connectedness to nature and to express deep gratitude for the trees and understories that give us life.' – Jo Wilmot

The exhibition Tall Trees and Understories will show at Fabrik, in Lobethal, South Australia, in 2020.

When I was invited, in my capacity as a poet, to be a part of Tall Trees and Understories, I began to collect the poems that I had already written on the theme of Solastalgia. The word was coined in 2005 by Glen Albrecht to refer to the distress specifically caused by environmental change. Of course I had poems that fitted with the theme. A bit more writing, and some help with ordering the mass (thank you, Graham Rowlands) and here is this book.

With changing climate, we will all feel solastalgia. Most of us, through changes in our personal environments, already have. What troubles us is not the building of a new supermarket where an old one was. It is almost always the loss of some natural feature that causes us distress. A loved tree, the sky above an empty field, these are places where the heart goes for rest, solace and rejuvenation.

We read of dystopian futures where no natural things exists, only buildings and highways, where one can no longer view the sky or touch a real petal. We see billions of dollars invested with the aim of living on Mars, as if that is easier than fixing the troubles on earth.

As I write this, the Amazon burns. Goodness knows what else will happen between now and the time you read this foreword. We are facing true disaster. However, I have great faith that the situation will be turned around. Eventually people will take the future into their own hands. There is so much each of us can do. And Anama (mentioned in this book) is not the only one planting trees.

Postscript: January 2020

Since I wrote the above, only three months ago, enormous tracts of Australia have burned, including the few acres where I have lived for a third of a century. We lost our home, our workshops, our studios, their contents, our tools and a lifetime of artworks. We escaped with our lives, our cars, our computers and our winter coats. Not much else.

We will rebuild on our scarred land. It will never be the same. We will continue to mourn it. But also we will watch the regeneration. After three weeks, there are already shoots at the base of a few of the gum trees.

I can only hope that people will insist that our leaders begin to lead for the betterment of all people and for the betterment of this sacred earth that we depend upon. I am optimistic and pessimistic at the same time. Goodness knows what will happen next.

I dedicate this book to people everywhere
who are planting, tending and protecting trees.

floats .... despite ...

the flight of the wild swan

between earth and air
between life and fire
between transcendence and the fragile body
between the wild swan and the burnt man
between divine ecstasy and nuclear fall out

the royal swan of the soul floats on the cosmic ocean
despite the cosmic ocean being filled with blood

a beak full of grubs

Blackbird in Honeysuckle

All these plants breathing
and turning sunshine to sugar
and thus you and I exist, my friend.

The blackbird is in the honeysuckle
with her shining eye and nest full of chicks.
How can I say I am more or less important

than her? Or the honeysuckle for that matter
or the pine tree wafting pollen or the wattle
with its blazing expression of sunshine.

Opposable thumbs and language don't make us
the Chosen even if ages ago we wrote that down
and believe it to this day. It doesn't make it true.

Do I really believe that some omnipotent creator
cares more about me than the giraffe, for example,
or something as hard-working and necessary as fungi?

The blackbird, in her mourning garb,
carries a beak full of grubs.
Her babies open their mouths like orchids.

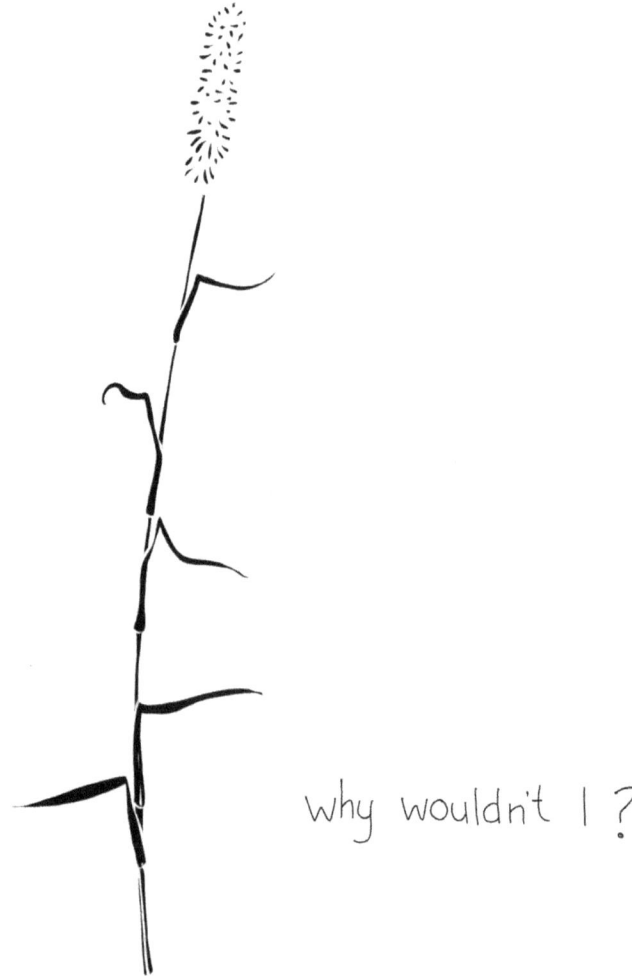

why wouldn't I ?

One Gift

If I could give you one gift, it would be this sunlight
lighting up these yellow grasses against this dark blue sky.
Why wouldn't I?

We all deserve some loving
and nothing in this world is so serious that these grasses
don't go on giving up their gasses.

Granted they're dying, but even death
is beautiful at the proper hour.
And heart-lift   is heart-lift   after all.

White Crow

The crow has turned white.
It's a dove now, cooing,
peaceful on the rooftop.

The doves have turned into magpies,
into eagles, into crows. Their eyes
are as indiscriminate as war.

People don't notice though.
People either have eyes of television
or eyes of distance over waves in good weather.

There is no coming back.
Not while the crow is white.
Not while doves are crows.

The Empty Man

I close my eyes
to the misplaced, the misunderstood,
the hollow eyes of the wronged.

I am a void.
I am a soil laid waste.
I am a landscape empty
and a howling wind.

But
I have buttons and baubles
and dollars and cents
that I traded for our inheritance.

weep tears, shed blood

salt wells
up through the ground
like vengeance

trees draw on it
crust themselves
white as driftwood
or bones

their once-song
is hollow
and echoey

instead
the wind
restless
relentless
heaps red dust in drifts
howls red dust in clouds

salt of my body
dust of my veins
weep tears
shed blood

we call it happiness

To God

You needed someone to
praise your good works. That's it.
That's why you created people,
so we could sing your praises
louder than birds on days like this
when spring takes off her jacket
and binds cheerful flowers into her hair.

Ah, beauty. We devour it,
are greedy for it. We call it happiness
or the face of a girl, or a well designed
television set or the legs of a millipede,
how they do the Mexican wave in miniature.

The world is full of it and we don't mind
if you created us to appreciate it;
someone has to appreciate works of art
and half the world's artists would
make their own audience if they could
and some of them do.

The trouble started when you let us believe
we were the centre of creation.
What were you doing, indulging us
or being insecure? In any case
we forgot that you exist (if you do exist)
our oh-so-clever minds working on
what beauty is or if there is any such thing.

Eventually we've decided that beauty
is a human construct, so you can
trot off home now, God. Sorry that
all your works are falling like trees in a forest,
that there is no one to hear them fall
but even if there were someone to hear
they'd have their earphones in.

I'm Angry with God Again

for filling mankind
with an inflated view
of its own importance:

'in My image,
go forth and multiply,
subdue the earth.'

And here we are,
having multiplied,
fighting each other for peace.

Having subdued the earth,
we're living in our own shit,
we're cooking ourselves under heaven.

And I can't remember God saying,
'subdue the weather.'
Let alone how.

earth and sap and air

Always Cockroaches

That I will someday
give my body to the earth
to the myriad creatures,
that my particles will become
earth and sap and air.
It seems apt.
I can delight in solitude
knowing I am not alone.
I can delight in the knowledge
of the teeming biome in my gut
or even that there are, apparently,
tiny creatures that live in my skin
that come out at night
and feed on my face.

Well, I am a biosphere.
I am an ecosystem.
I am diversity and interconnectedness,
a habitat.
I am a *homo sapiens*,
a small upright animal standing
on an earth in crisis,
a tiny creature feeding on its face.

What will the earth do
with this weird domineering creature
that seems hell-bent on destruction?
She will allow it of course,
knowing it will purge itself.
And will humans destroy every last thing?
Hardly. There's always cockroaches
and whatever it is that feeds on their faces.

hard to believe things flew!

reminiscence from a barren planet

glass sky
wind like an itch
we walk barefoot over stones
over earth laid bare

there once was a thing called soil
it was made of fine particles of rock crushed
over aeons

life had such urge back then
that mosses grew and grasses
lichen and trees
and their dead crumbled fibrous into soil
and animals came

at first small things:
insects, worms, but later
scaled creatures and winged!
hard to believe, things flew!

creatures of enormous size also
were supported and nurtured by soil
and by water falling
pure from clouds

the fireball sun was a god in those days
golden and soft

plants turned their leaves towards it
as if listening

nothing faces it now
nothing can

how can they grow to be giants?

after fire, Katarapko

the old river flows
deep and slow
like memory

it hides its scars
in a floating lace
of water weed

fire raged here
leapt up and ate trees:
giants of time

amongst the blackened corpses
saplings tremble
fragile as dragonfly wings

how can they grow to be giants
in this era
of fire?

Our Hold on the Planet

after Robert Frost's poem of the same name

Robert Frost in a hey-ho mood
thinks Nature is enamoured of mankind,
a little bit in favour, one percent or so.
His evidence is how our numbers grow.

Are spawned more likely, a fungus, a disease,
or that's the way I see it – clearly,
in sharper focus now no mist can rise
below the baking sun, the hollow sky.

Crops die, ice melts, temperatures soar,
whole populations starve and some with more
dole out just a little, just enough
to make them feel most generous.

Meanwhile, factories belch out the smoke
on which the world proceeds to choke.
If I were Nature, I don't reckon I'd be pleased
with my disease.

I'd be thinking to diminish human numbers –
perhaps the odd small natural disaster?

Sketching Drought

Sketch tree-lined creeks as squiggles.
Draw the roads with a T-square.
Cut square pieces out in grids
and call them paddocks.
Water them with something.
Ink is good; you can use green or yellow.
Most likely they'll fade anyway
to grey or ochre, earth pigment.
That's if the sky doesn't blow them away.
As for those creeks, they used to be dark –
undiluted sepia, tea without milk.
Now they are the colour of split peas
or dirt. There's an awful lot of dirt.
It's escaping. It's not on the ground.

Little Snatch of Darkness

Clouds close over the sun like eyelids.
The darkening contains a crow.
He's rattling in his throat
and even though I love him and his blue eye,
the sound is black.

I have a table
especially for the crows.
There I place my meat scraps
and they come picking,
speaking in dark words
and glinting.

O singer of elegies,
when I'm dead
you're welcome to pick my bones.
I'd like to whiten them under the sun
so you can perch there
and sing your rattly songs
and be a little snatch of darkness
in my day.

their lovesick dance

two gods

every morning oblivious
the TV wails its terrible tales
of blood and money
and ego and fear

and every morning
the sun roars up from the east
bringing with him
the dance of chlorophyll
as all our plant allies
turn their faces towards him

and every morning
we breakfast the breakfast
we owe to them
being as we are entirely dependent
on their lovesick dance
just this side of chaos

and every evening
the sun slips behind the hill
full faced honest
lighting up the opposite hill
in the brightest of orange hope

and every evening oblivious
the TV wails its terrible tales
of blood and money
and ego and fear

Owl at Dusk

When the owl circled me
I was standing in the garden
with my fists full of beans.
It was too dark to pick them anymore
and I was just standing there
breathing in the scent
of bean sap and bright earth.

The owl flew around me three times
with its face of eyes,
and close, within arms' reach.
I couldn't keep up, nor wanted to.
I couldn't make sense of it, nor wanted to.
And then he perched close by
and chittered to his wife,
and before they flew off
he did it again, both of us turning circles,
me on my dizzy feet, he on his lift of wing.

People have given me all sorts of explanations
as they are wont to do, but no matter.
We looked into each other's eyes for a while,
that's all.
I don't know what he saw in mine
apart from astonishment and awe,
but I looked into eyes
that make sense of darkness.

I keep my tealeaves in bags
just in case

Not Looking for Signs

I'm not looking for signs
but a hundred crows
flew out of that tree
one after the other for
five minutes, like autumn
leaves in a stiff southerly.

And now the moon has come up
as bloody as an orange.
It's smoke in the upper atmosphere,
you say. I say blood is blood.
Smoke is blood. The black char
of fires on the face of the moon is blood.

I'm not looking for signs.
I keep my tea leaves in bags just in case.
I never use salt or if I do I never spill it.
Cover the mirrors.
Goodness knows what you'd see
in the dead of night from the light

of a moon like that.

soundless

impossible spring

with thanks to Dorothy Hewett

mean
with urgency
the days

soundless
I open and close
my mouth

wafting
insomnia
spring

drifting
through pine pollen
my breathless mind

this paradise
is full green and mad
its terrible taste

prickling skin
I salivate
a different tune

moonlight
I stalk
with death

hopeful songs

my heart believes
with the simplicity of a wren
that rain will come

maybe these high lines of white
will draw it in

the bush holds its breath

for some it comes too late

the banksia in autumn orange
is bruised beyond repair

likewise the wattle bares its black teeth
and the bluegums in the gorge
sing their death songs
through runnels of dried sap

but the dear old burly stringybarks
wait with their hearts in their roots

the native orchids also
pulse faintly beneath the mulch

and wren and I sing

hopeful songs

Summer Dream

I dreamed of the sun hanging
as red as earth in the morning sky.
It was the hottest summer ever.
Crows gathered in huge numbers
as if they were expecting something.

We slept under wet sheets, tossed and tangled
with dreams stacked on dreams like
animals in a children's story but atop
the rooster, a crow called its dire warning.

The grass dried and turned to tinder.
Trees fleshed themselves pure white.
Their tatters of bark clacked like rhythm sticks
in the relentless northerly wind.

In between we tossed in our sleep
dreamed of flame, of running immobile.
Great old trees died on the ridges
and stood, grey and bony.
Crows murdered there like huge black flowers.

In that season the sky was never blue.
Stars were hidden by dust and smoke
but towards morning the faintest breath
blew up from the south, carrying the scent
of something we remembered from long before,

something we wished for without knowing
what it was we wished for: the scent of rain.

survival and love

Adelaide Hills, January 2015

The northerly was thick
with ash and smoke.
Cinders fell on tinder bush.
Our rickety house stood
as if waiting, as if cowering
amongst trees that evolved to burn,
that thrashed in erratic gusts of heat.
We fled, carrying papers and mementoes,
medicines and photos, survival and love.

Came back next day to an untouched home
and took up rakes as water bombers flew
their endless rounds, and teams of men and women
continued their brave fight, went in yellow,
came back black, sooty, and tired,
to rest and eat before moving in again.

Everyone watched the weather maps:
possible rain preceded by high winds
and dry lightning: lightning that poured
like rivers to the ground and raised
tendrils of smoke, sirens and fear.

Then rain, meaningful rain,
the scent of wet dirt and ash,
and our hearts settled
like moisture does
down the roots of trees
to the deep, still, quiet earth.

Meeting the Spirit of the River Murray

She was standing on the water. She said,
'It's OK. Spirits can.'
The river around her was calm and silvery,
as if early dawn was the colour of moonlight
or moonlight cast no shadows.
Mist rose from the water like breath.

I said that I would have expected the spirit of a river,
especially this river, The Murray,
so wide and sluggish, to be an old man.
She said, 'My form changes. I'm a spirit after all.'

Well, you'll be pleased to know, I apologised from us all
for the junk in the water, the dams and barricades,
the poisons, the fertilisers,
the broken glass along her banks for miles,
the European carp felling trees,

that her flow is so diminished,
that people suck her dry,
that her mouth to the wide ocean, is cankered and still.
She nodded, then smiled and said
so calmly, 'It is my business to flow.'

I told her how much I love the river,
the scent of it at night, all the life it nurtures:
the massive gum trees, tiny herbs, the myriad birds,
dragonflies with wings finer than a breeze.
I could have cried for the love of it.

I said how pleased I am now to see the floodwater
spreading in the flat lands, over the grey, grey mud flats,
watering the dying trees, the brittle tangle of lignum.
'Mind you,' I said, 'the mosquitoes! So many you breathe them.'
She said, 'My business is to flow.'

I said I hoped that the floods upstream,
devastating as they were for people,
may eventually do some good,
may eventually reach the sea.
Whereat she nodded again and said,
'It is my business to flow.'

the brittle tangle of lignum

each day
 the simplest of things

Each Day

Each day
the simplest of things

The quick body of a honeyeater
neat as an evening suit
sipping, supping, flitting and twittering

All the petals have fallen from the plum tree
Now it unfurls leaves as soft as babies' palms

On the far ridge
still
tree skeletons stand

Clouds come and go
like days, like seasons, like years

The rose stands in its own thorns
and adds more leaf to last year's brave branches

Politics and problems go on in the world of man
hate   and horror   and greed
each day

But each day rabbits nibble fresh grass
and each day
the simplest of things

walked all day
with acorns in his pockets

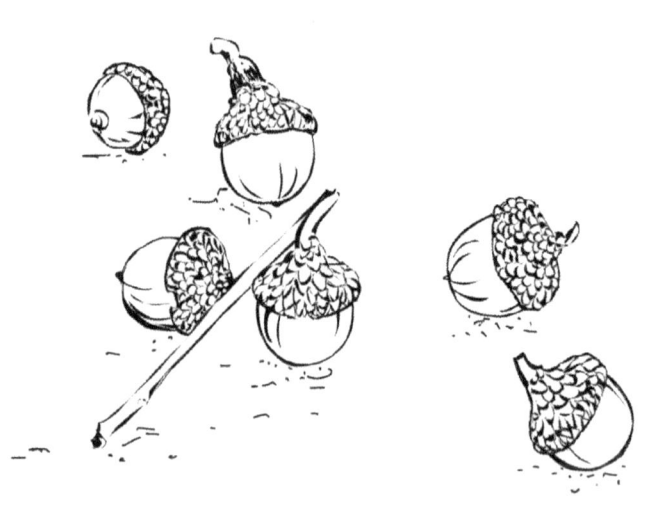

Come Forest

(for Anama who is growing one)

The man who planted trees
walked all day with acorns in his pockets,
dibbled them into the ground and a forest sprouted.
The clouds came back. The weather changed.

I have a friend who is planting a forest.
She has some acres and plans it well.
First rids the place of brambles and other weeds.
She's nestling in the seedlings, thousands of them.
A hundred hopeful people help.

Imagine these plants, like Europeans in a strange land,
a place arid of connections.
But perhaps the land remembers:
ancestors of these trees once grew here.

Come rain, come wind, come sunshine!
Bring them strength and providence!

A few years, a few deaths, and much growth later
these trees shimmy around your hips
your waist, your shoulders.
Shining with youth, they move towards maturity.
They change the weather.

Come forest, come forest, come forest.

in your hand

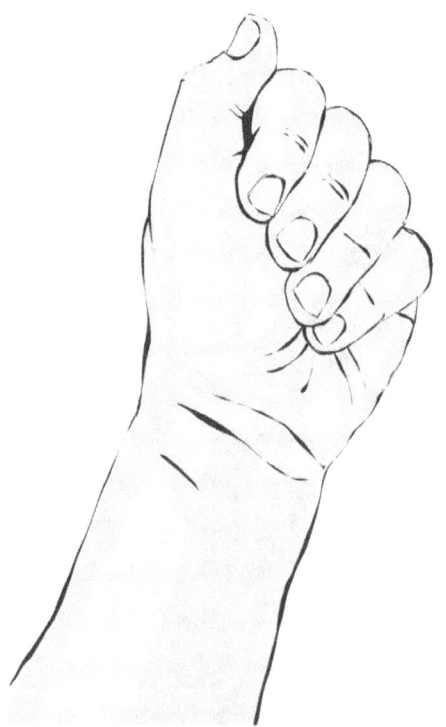

What the Dreamed Man Gave

The dreamed man opens your hand,
into it he sprinkles something,
closes your fist and says, 'This is Mundus.'
Here, in your hand is Mundus
and Mundus is the earth, the cosmos, everything.
You have a little pinch of everything in your hand.
Separate yourself if you can.

Now I ask you
where is your tiny self with all its fears and irritations?
Where is your desire for the next pair of shoes,
the next piece of art, the next love, the next lust?
Where are your concerns
of war and peace, of living and dying,
joy, your friend's joy,
pain, your friend's pain,
politicians and their hollow words?
I ask you, what are these things,
what are all these separate things,
when here
in your hand
is Mundus?

Here in your hand are your ancestors, your neighbour,
your daughter, your daughter's daughter,
all the ages of man, Venus of Willendorf, crones and bones.
You hold in your hand the nervous magpie bearing worm.
You hold in your hand the rain and next year's rain,
the dust blowing over the deserts,
the very earth spewing rock and that rock
flowing like blood down mountainsides of its own creation.

You hold the spark of life,
the myriad beings, the seed, the tree,
the fragile microcosm of the cell,
photosynthesis, the sun, the sun, the great sun.

For Mundus is the heavens also,
is the earth rolling through blankness carrying you
and your handful.
It is silent space out to the edges of nowhere,
contained in all time from the beginning-without-end
and the end birthing beginnings – forever, forever.
God-dust it is, right here, in your hand.
Come now, would you baulk?
Would you baulk when
this little bit of Mundus in your hand is
you,
is all you have ever loved?
You have to take the large with the small;
just because you are afraid is no reason to deny it.

What will you name it?
The first spark of light,
the first-ever nudge of movement.
It is the almost-silent reverberating first word.
It is the beginning. It is the end.
It is that there is no beginning and no end.
And I ask you, how do you put it down?
For it is Mundus
and there is a sprinkle of it
in your hand.

Unexpected Lecture on Global Warming from a Bird

This morning a Brown Treecreeper
tapped on the window.
'Wake up!' he said.
But I was already awake because
he'd been tapping on the mirror
of the van in which I'd been sleeping
since it was light enough to see.

Perhaps you don't know the brown treecreeper.
He hops around on the ground,
quite game, pecking at goodness knows what,
tiny things, insects, ants.
And he shimmies up tree trunks with his weird legs
as if there was no such thing as gravity.

Anyhow, when he tapped on the window beside my face,
he said, 'Wake up! It's time to wake up.'
And added, as if it was unimportant,
'Wake up to this beautiful world.
Save it. Save us. Save yourself.'

all day, these days, from his high twig

The Original Song

Such a small bundle of darkness to produce such light,
the clean, clear notes tumble all day, these days,
from his high twig.

He came into the world
with the song he sings, this blackbird.
Who knows what he feels?

We came bearing a song also,
but have forgotten it,
replaced it with a lament.

The lament is about suffering.
I expect to sing it for the rest of my life.
I expect to hear it from every voice.

In another room, my loved one
watches videos and cries.
Beauty makes him cry, as does kindness.

Well, we all cry about kindness as if it was unusual.
We cry about breaking through boundaries, overcoming trials.
We cry about hope. These are our laments.

But what if our essential song is a song of joy?
What if our song is as simple as the blackbird's?
And what if, suddenly, we all remember it

and sing?

what matters

fresh food
love and its confusion
pure water and pure air
vegetables for breakfast
laughter for lunch
whiskey for dinner

sometimes the mind
troubles its troubles
agitates its worry beads
then in comes a small grey bird
singing
into the dispassionate air

the song
dies and dies and dies
and is sung and sung and sung
and the body whose ear hears this song
is a little elevated, a little less
bound to the earth

that's the thing
about small grey birds –
they matter

A Transparent Matter

In the morning sunshine,
the hop bush breaks
into angles of colour and tone.

I would like to paint
so that light shines through.
Transparency seems to be
the nature of everything.
We are ninety-eight per cent
nothing, so physics says:
waves and particles,
in and out of the boxes
we make of reality.
It all seems so solid
but from now
to now, are we matter?
Are we energy?

And that goes for you,
my son, my loving poltergeist,
my formless one.
Here is the world you loved:
form and matter, waves and particles,
angles of green in the hop bush,
and light that shines through.

Blue Wren Fights His Reflection

When Blue Wren fights his reflection,
put your face up close to the window,
his sharp bits on the other side.
He is like an attack of moths.
He is action in blue brilliance behind sharp claws.

You can't say, 'This blue is like…'
and metaphor the autumn sky or summer sea,
or give it a name, 'azure' perhaps –
there is no other blue like this.

It is blue-wren blue and not another type of blue.
Except, perhaps, between blue wrens
where, 'My blue is better than your blue
and my wives love me, and will not leave me,
so you can go away! Buzz off! Flap, flap!'

It must be confusing to Blue Wren
that his enemy will not back down,
is so hard and unyielding, and yet obviously
so much weaker, never striking a blow.

Or perhaps by now, he knows exactly
who he is fighting. Perhaps he fights to see
how well he fights, strutting
and flexing, practising his moves.

Maybe he hopes his wives are watching
but, knowing wives, after a cursory glance
in his direction, they are more interested
in talking amongst themselves, gossip perhaps,
or philosophy, or whatever the wives
of Blue Wren might twitter about.

Oh Blue Wren, Little Target, Little Body of Will,
Little Fury, Little Burst of Air, Little Puffer,
Little Ferocious Heart, may you inflate with pride.
Your enemy will not unwife you. Your enemy
is flatter than a grandmother on a summer's day.

his enemy will not back down

in the green unfocused world

in the waterhole

you slide into your reflection
hair floating in the green unfocused world

the sound of water
of blood pumping

you are alone, pink and naked
half welcomed, half spurned

the depths are cold and ancient
dark with some unknown fear

an eel perhaps with ragged teeth
you surface gasping

your hair is pasted to your scalp
the tannin tuts in your mouth

tea trees crouch around the edges
as if they are telling secrets

www.ingramcontent.com/pod-product-compliance
Lightning Source LLC
Chambersburg PA
CBHW062201100526
44589CB00014B/1897